IDIOGEST

IDIOGEST

Ed Taylor

BlazeVOX [books]

Buffalo, New York

publisher of weird little books

BlazeVOX [books]

blazevox.org

2   4   6   8   0   9   7   5   3   1

B   X

Acknowledgments

Texts here previously appeared in the chapbook *Rubaiyat of Hazmat* (BlazeVox Books), *Double Room, Elimae, Exquisite Corpse, Knock, Mississippi Review Online, New Writing* (UK), *Nth Position* (UK), *RealPoetik, Sentence, Slipstream, Slope, Square One, The Quarterly, The 2ndHand, XCP: Cross Cultural Poetics,* and the exhibit "Card Catalog Poetry," Buffalo State College (Buffalo, NY).

Contents/Idiogest

Genesis...13

Juju...14

Parable...15

Religious Poem...16

Ant On A Rothko..17

Resurrection..18

Eohippus...21

Roaches..23

"Rapture Of The Bees"..24

Droit De Seigneur...25

Deer Park..26

My Amygdla..27

Journalism 101...28

Hitler's Yacht...29

Historiography..30

The Big Tent..31

Civic Duty...32

Misocainea..33

Daytime Emmy..34

Swim Lesson..35

Mystery Of Perseverance..36

Tokyo Swimming Pool...37

12-Tone Tune...38

Hamtramck..39

Music Sutra...40

Artist..41

Contemporary Music...42

Perspective: Torment..43

"Save Me Or I'll Kill You" (Love Song).......................44

Metaphysical Still Life...45

In My Dream 46

Tropical Storm 47

Depression 48

Bulletin 49

Institutional View 50

Pilgrim 51

Scene From A Bus 52

Off Broadway 53

Real Estate 54

Backseat Driver 55

Manhattan Sutra 56

Still Life With Insomnia & Tokyo 57

Easter In The Horse Latitudes (Capriccio) 58

Pure Word 59

Aubade 60

Sargasso Sea 61

Separation Anxiety 62

Punch And Judy 63

Still Life With Guilt 64

Dream Fragment 65

Cold Spring 66

Laughing Sutra 67

O, I have suffered
with those that I saw suffer

—Miranda, *The Tempest*

language is less about memory
than about sutures

—Ricardo Pau-Llosa

Dedicated to Seth

GENESIS

Label maker. That's god.
Maxi with wings.

Early times bourbon, a catcher on rye, a pitcher with jug ears.
A dream team.

"International paper puts the tree in tree frog," the announcer
                                                    reads.
Then strike three; caught with a snake in your hand.

Next stop Cannibalopolis, father-son holy roast with aristocrats,
inbred as setters.

A bipolar wife's by your side. Her name is Dawn
& she's a knockout.

Put up your dukes.

JUJU

on Shinnecock a lone trapper
mailing address for mind-body correspondence
discretion from creatures without mouthpieces
no miracles after all, just this world of grease
for Jesus
electricity like balm to spiked ears
snakes and ladders
batter for cake and wife
the option-encrusted throne o'god
bracing for dust

PARABLE

Today: Sirens. Lungs of clay. Lamb. Lamp.
Remembered things that ride with death, the great cease fire, the
end of hostilities. The paraclete fumbles for the gun-shaped
Zippo.

Homeland Security holds hands at a séance but only
silence rises, a code: a turncoat only bones when it's over.

Jesus kisses toads on plates of gold. Oro pro nobis.
Noblesse oblige, my liege. Then saints march in, argue, demand
discounts. The supreme court rules and yawns.

A guy in yellow kayak sentenced to ride waves in the
gorge where the water's stopped. The needle of boat sews the
green lips shut. They will not close. The trout watch open
mouthed wild things in air, the dam's intelligent design, evolving.

RELIGIOUS POEM
glossolalia

Slaves unearth a whale in Alabama cotton.
North, spring snow piles like white dirt around
one Hispanic
                    who "had" a psychotic episode,
ran a road naked & verily in wilderness
was he naked & in the deep night stole he
a canoe & paddled he the canoe down a river's
middle leaving Roman posses to swim for him.
                                     All this
comes in a Greek dream of breakfast with two
women in rehab & one goes I've seen her age
ya know & she's seen me age ya know
                    & somehow
we stir coffee with small bones, waking
cloud leviathans drifting high, their
deep pleadings a sonar of love,
                        voices,
a chorus rewarding an audience
with comedy & tragedy as it watches
angels fall, their wings dying, for to be
found & wept over, their black coats white
with lime & hair reaching for the clay
bed to be forever shared with the scared
& hopeful, immigrants to a promised
land where white bolls of stars
are harvest

ANT ON A ROTHKO
Albright Knox Art Gallery, Buffalo NY

After flat years of gray a wall, and one direction left, a climb
turning orange and turning yellow in the teeth of white like a
frame. Then a big wind like breath pressed me to loosen my only
hold, whispering pictures of French meat, and, my people, I
finally understood God.

RESURRECTION

you take one step in a field
watch a foal at hay
stiff & twitching

two things: caulking a hull
& caulking a hull

three meals a day and a ray
of orchard

four white balls in a lotto drawing
bobbing like bottles with messages

five smart guys stick their hands in hives
& get stuck in honey

six ways from Sunday to Monday

seven & seven equals too weak to fight
the waves of waves

eight is a NASCAR event
an eternity of left turns & a loud crowd
pulling right like an oar

cat of nine tails twitching
missing its absent owners who left it
outside

wren-10-tin come in from the code
this cold is still a killer

double ones eleven chopsticks for copycats
the news hour

at twelve take a first step away from the edge
the black car at the curb & you now willing

to walk where you are going

ICTHYOSTEGA
first four-legged creature in the world, from fossils in
eastern Greenland
9/11/2005

Everyone here in cave city is pale. All the houses are coal
black. At evening we sit outside to watch their eyes open and
close. Our street is a fish, silversided. Doors let their tongues
hang but neighbors do not talk.

Whispers of fossils filter up. We claw at the ground, earth
in teeth, but not fast enough.

Meanwhile something gleaming struggles from dark water
onto the slick bank, born above us.

EOHIPPUS

Dim attention to its ten legs,
may be paid by early crowds
on the sold-out savannah.
                        Now it is nine,
Sixto Lezcano played outfield
without opposable thumbs, what
who said that, hustle that charlie
out of here, we're serious and placing
bets.
                Eight stable lads lathering
each other in a downpour equals
a Greek scene way too late. Ouch,
that's healing with vengeful
liniment.
                    Seven times the legs come
down but the order is not correct yet.
Windows shutting, nobody welcome.
                              Wait
a damn minute, for six eons we've
put up with the chase and are tired,
stop trotting, you'll confuse
the track.
                  Pentagon equals a five-
sided figure, a crystal gift
for a runner up.
                        I think four
philosophies concerning spontaneous
generation would fit nicely right
about now.
               Those trees skirted
by fire alone with its three hobbies,
water, air, and theories.
                           Can we ken
the extreme intent with which the two
inspectors loaded the cannon bone
with gelignite, giggling?

                              One perfect
egg, one perfect plate, and a perfect
knife for the perfect surgeon.
                                        At no time
should you leave your seat. Now it's time
for thunder, running, mad dash to freedom
across the frontier. It has begun.

After the big bang, a pinata
and pony rides for the kids.

ROACHES

The night today is thin.
See through it.
Behind one star is just another,
late again.
              This
happens every day,
it seems.
         There is confusion
concerning time,
who should be where
& why.
Am I awake, asleep,
burned by reentry
or launch.

The jets fly high.
In the foxhole the fox.
A scar of horizon,
blade of sun dull enough.

Spare us one more day.
It is busy here
when the light snaps
off.

"RAPTURE OF THE BEES"
evangelicals' explanation of colony collapse disorder

some believe jesus whistles
      or something

& the bee grains drain up
for duty, which would be
        what, why?

the answer is curtain. mystery
closes the show & him thanked
      from the wings

for not sparing the rod
& outside roses

are red, violets are blue,
sugar is sweet, for a few

final gardens before the fall
falls
       & nothing gets up

DROIT DE SEIGNEUR

The bolls of light harvested

If you make me know something
is that sex

The monster comes daily
taking what the village
still gives

Every night like a necklace
Broken the pieces scatter-
ed

In water it can
disappear the rain
a depth
        like sun

Blue green white
a page a day
Travel in shadow
Deep fur
a knowing

Cold is coming
a king

Bow before you speak
creature

DEER PARK
after Wang Wei

The self is an intermittent neurosis
   —Michel Houellebecq

   I can't think about that now, must drag daughter to
audition, a cairn of stones, Ramsey Lewis or Ramses, Karen or
Hatin', an unaccompanied sonatina for tendons, the elk like fog.
   I see the nerves in the earth, the trees reach out to squeeze
life from the sky, birds cackle from the thorns of beaks, and my
car hull uncrackable, the nut safe inside, carrying out orders, food
and assassination in the memos, a field of memos and a bank
wrecked ahead, one wheel spinning.
   On the bridge a Buddhist whirls, the prayers come around
and scatter in fear at the scat of a dragon on armatures of serene
bones.
   I fix things and move.
   There is a beautiful bag of darkness and deep in it
something curls or furls, a flag of leaf waiting for 10,000 feet of
clear air, the constant pilgrims drifted to the shoals of beds and
the tide a far-gone conclusion.
   I am taller than when I started. I imagine I'll eat.
   The world gets, after the bad weather of science, its life
back.

MY AMYGDLA

It is the finale of Harry Potter & hope.
Our century's over so get in line.
The bottom of the Fruit Loops bowl

looks good now that bomb shelters
burst with action items for EBay.
Where to run when the finish rubs
                              off?

Every year a sturgeon trying to fly
dents a Floridian while the Xavante
pole Amazon dugouts & reach for

even a dial-up connection but catch
only fish (maybe Cameron Diaz can
                              help).
Teeth of DNA, ladder of DNA,

treasure map of DNA, all end
& begin in the egg on your plate,
sunny side lost in sports talk until

it walks on skinny fins from the eating
& the world can't find its theory
of mind, the scrambled lovey-dovey,

evo-devo of choosing where to sit &
why to waltz, when to fool that some
of the people, who to groom, & how

to stay inside the tribe, as outside
is wild with stranger tigers.

JOURNALISM 101

Meet my sportswriter covered in grass, she's a doe with
headlights. These manufacturing reports, those bullets of sugar,
them mounds dem bones; our Ruhr under fire. Dispatch a shuttle
mission into the inner ear. A vote for concealed weapons and
wine, dear wine, AND I don't care, says Chinese nation to the
evil within, give me hydroelectric dams of love. What evolves out
of electricity: this is not the first you've heard of it, surely. May I
suggest hunger before takeoff makes whites whiter and you can
save this child or you can not, just don't spoil the epidemic
(world takes a wait and see attitude). Going nowhere? Can I get a
lift?

HITLER'S YACHT

*Homicide is not a sin. It is sometimes a necessary
violence on resistant and ossified forms of existence which
have ceased to be amusing.*
Bruno Schulz

Hitler's yacht is in the attic upside down.
Hitler's yacht is a violin. It was a gift from birds.

Hitler's yacht is a crumb of ash on a mustache.
Hitler's yacht wears glasses, limps, left a husband
at the altar, eats sugar from the bowl.

The rusty tears of Hitler's yacht sink like stones
in black earth down to where the bones eat.

Hitler's yacht sleeps & sighs. The wind has died.

HISTORIOGRAPHY

A world of wistful mistake
& delicate error; some thing young, hunted.

Driven to frantic escape it breaks a leg, waits
for blunt force, the surgery of mercy now history.

That sound is hounds. The doctor is out.
Traumerai. Trauma.
Drama.

A falcon dead on a sidewalk.
Eleven episodes & an option for more.

A prose of equations. The answers:
a license to fly by night, eyes, shut,
on the prize. Life by the numbers.

An empty hive veiled by spiders.

THE BIG TENT

Divide, do not unite; win a prize. Offer sugared pennants.
Guess weight & fate. Spin until dizzy in blinding light.
Bleating & shrieks rise like fireworks.

Time & menu: Jurassic on a stick. Now something
crawls the midway backwards: a torn dress, empty
by the Cinderella ride to the long hall, the corn palace,
where the dead harvest stares from glass, & animals
lie under flies.

The freaks close their robes, open smokes.
It is finished here. Pull up stakes, leave the holes behind.

CIVIC DUTY

take off coffee & lost lunch
      lady of Spain with a spaniel on
      this morning of many handles—
you are Keats with a vengeance
five miles of hardtack & Russell Crowe's sabre-
toothed Oscar clout beats me to the punch
so I have to make amends losing again
      there is a hum in the world
      have to get that fixed
after rain refuge shadows falling before they can stand
brutal in here & outside
oy don't ask

if losing it is good as having it
               why write
what is included in the fixed price

here paint faces off like duellists
& the hand points but we bite the fingers
         yellow envelope white page bird in a rage
         a tisket a tasket a Greek and smelly
                    tragedy

to Mao American brands were sugar-
coated bullets, but little did he know
the apple smooth thighs of our groceries

hell is a hell of a place says the captain
for whom you assume the position
till further notice
      & the voting for top
      rogue cop
      is over

MISOCAINEA

from Greek: hatred of anything new

And among other things, the poor pigeons, I perceive,
were loth to leave their houses, but hovered about the
windows and balconies, till they some of them burned
their wings and fell down.
> Diary of Samuel Pepys, September 2, 1666, the
> day of the Great Fire of London

The cat's diet, coffee and butterflies. Now the animal
startles at her heartbeats. On the porch the quartet watches the
cat knot. They drink tea and whiskey. They practice, knitting
bands of static. They call it friendship, wear it like protection.
    Things get trapped and stuck. Sun rattles into its hole.
Bingo. Beach Boys on the radio, fading. Car wheels like roulette.
The quartet bets and keeps playing, while it gets blurry outside.
Taking no chances, the music gets sinister. Loud. No one hears
the wire tightening. The four loosen their collars.

DAYTIME EMMY

the curtains hang like careless patriots
the gray of street your hair & eyes
you smoke too much & go to seed
      the coming of mail like omens today
      that blue man a shadow you dodge
the boy of your future meets the girl
                    of your past
today their child will die in your arms
or you will watch TV & sleep
you hide in the light & prepare to fight
that rumble below is only a signal
the final cable laid in ground—
anatomy lesson
     a truth to be found
     turn down the sound

SWIM LESSON

the water cold as algebra

the live float as if dead
the young old & blue

a thin knitter fattens waiting
& waiting for a child to come
                              out

a teacher up to her neck
puts glasses back on
as the thrashing stops
at the deep end
                    finally

MYSTERY OF PERSEVERANCE
for Fernando Pessoa

What is going on outside. Is there jousting. What horns blow. Why. Are there clouds & sounds. Former. Previous to.

Alleviated septum no longer bound by anatomy free to divide the sky. Ha. A small yoke. Some thing making easier the haul uphill what is dug from earth.

TOKYO SWIMMING POOL
for Chris Marker

Louis Armstrong seeps into blue through aquatic Hitachi speakers. Guests celebrate marriage for an hour around it before filing to a van for the next client. It is a house with water floor. Out of respect it is ignored. In white gloves an old man skims limp maple leaves, dreaming of a woman's nape and today's mushrooms, a taste like clouds, nothing.

12-TONE TUNE

Shout at the sun, leave burned and alone. Maybe if a land rose: moaning hot pavement corsets, fur burning corn, a ten, sand tea.

There are no more Adelaides. The river walks on thin legs, around the world and back. Capture the flag sound, a ripping in wind. Fling the vast oiled musculature of a conservative street. Get ripped as a sniggler: flat as the lake wind in braids, a joke buzzer oil rig. Pick and choose.

Win, die deeper, plant seed in mud, rutting a tower of water. It stands and falls on silver feet. Hello little paisley Pekingese, it is time for the 50s. One more time.

At podiums, conductors whistle trains to stops and musicians walk into morning war where art is worse than Stukas. Must type watching the keys or you end out of tune. Lose either way. The blues.

HAMTRAMCK
fantasia

your majesty de jure spare parts for Cuba
Rudys foot the bill at every reckoning because
                                            they are there like Everest
what is all this? Genuine Nazi dinnerware or not? I see the Pope
slide into second and the ballet shifty in an alley naked
for every four corners there are five times the pain relief you get
                                                                with child
a mandrake the magician in every bodega like a bay of pigs and
Belorus now is aground off Miami anxious
                              as limpet mines in the museum of lost time
                              like ten minutes you waste every day
                              to pray
                              for another arm or two a long neck
a leg blah blah capitalism etc. and the other inconvenient viruses
                                            a bad case
                                            of cracked DNA
mean cars won't turn over their saucy pipes to the air
wives hunker down when transmission's in reverse
                                                  it hurts
word gets out that it doesn't start and next thing you know it's
slow slow slow then stop giving up the body in a corner going for
                              broke
                              instead of fixed
it is a disease these trees see every Kokomo hangdog pitchfork
                                                  season
out of gas closed for space shuttle docking see you in spring
                                            yeah right
between the eyes votes
                        the city – it is official

MUSIC SUTRA

My instructor's a famous drunk,
missing teeth where a bridle would fit,
expertise like coolant in his tubes
but not enough to do the job.
We sit in a blue room in his suburban ranch.
To save something there is no light.
When he finally speaks—you know the difference
between pigeon and morning dove?—
he looks like John Adams the elder
and leads me to a window, saying
"play what you see." A woman in a wheelchair,
lots of fried things, a hospitality suite,
a bus without wheels. I offer a G major scale
greased with irregular screeches,
stomp my foot and hit him with the instrument,
which splinters. For god's sake, he says.

I'll clean up, I say, but he's fiddling
with his ponytail. This isn't some poem,
he says, this is serious. You messed up
my hair. I can teach you no more.
Then he slaps me on the back,
says, have you eaten? Let's
celebrate.

ARTIST

you lay it down
drop the bamboo brush
its bristles eyelash black

in the window of sky a spider
many stories
in air

where is the web
where is
where

like the Chinese monk
flies between mountains
you leave the room

empty hands open
a thread of light
in the sun

where you were

CONTEMPORARY MUSIC

"I may no longer look forward to Paradise
the immortal pleasure of being left alone."

Waiter, there's soup in my fly.
No reprieve for the species.

The neighbors decided
your abbatoir needs paint.

Mayday mayday, the communists
cried, going down.

Bull elk ride salespeople
to war college for fishermen,
everyone late.

What does this leave us?
This down-filled bag of life,
this sceptered isle,
this angleland.

PERSPECTIVE: TORMENT

three is a torrent in my book
even if they are veiled women

a couplet or a cutlet
sweet potato pie to die for

avoidance & denial survive
even the spin cycle

as if life is a tumor &
every day another cell

this room filled with browned flowers
an Eden until the cows come home

perfumed linen handkerchief or scent bottle
how do you avoid today

give me a playoff game & some hope
for overtime

let the hurricanoes rage
it is all just water under the fridge

defrosting
on de cake

"SAVE ME OR I'LL KILL YOU" (LOVE SONG)

> *Sálvame o te mato*
> —shooting victim to surgeon
> New York Times 12/5/08

Unetherized on a cold table with drain—
is this doctor or coroner caressing the body,
both naked under pale light in an odd operation?

There are no tools.
Nothing steel and clean in this empty theater,
where students see the drama of devotion,
the oldest story, where someone pledges
a quest, to find heart and hold it
from the dogs around
outside always.

You in the mask,
your head a black hole in the white,
your skin my accident, my crash—
to you I am delivered, a sad package,

but I have a hand left with which to plead, to reach
for your throat, no longer patient,
lover

METAPHYSICAL STILL LIFE

A scientist, old brass, a painting, hay.
The coarse tongue of river
fills a mouth. At the zoo the otter
and sea lion dry as smoke. Some
Bathsheba in a sun dress. Tree
branch, antler. Crows in a black eye
of cloud closing.

IN MY DREAM

my head spills
across the pillow like pooled paint,
all of me flat as the sheets after,
slow as a patient lover,
the leak.

I can't stand finally for or against anything, just lie

& lie till the night nurse with needles again sneaks in,
not wanting to wake me, but huffing, clumsy.
A current of whispers stirs her hair.
My hair.

I fake sleep,
make it easy & she rams home her version of things,
a dose of the pricks,
hundreds it seems, millions.

Her sharps she dumps, chum for the trash
cans gathering at her legs.

The medicine hits its mark.

I drift up round, near the fixture in a necklace of bubbles,
pearls brighter than lights
dead now,

but already the soft hiss again,
the slow yaw over the holes below
choked with spikes swimming,
clicking against the cans.

TROPICAL STORM

the umbrella dusted
with light
black teeth gleam
two babies laugh
from their mountaintops

diamond house

pennant of smoke
a room full of people
everything cancelled
in the wild air

sleep children
someone whispers
waking
a screamer

DEPRESSION

in spite of the weather you say it's your birthday
                but rain in all corners of the universe
I do not believe in the helping strategy
                or reading aloud to the elderly
don't trust them don't trust them they leak like the *Times*
                however eiderdown's in my book a myth
(the ducks have a different story)
                it remains cold here in rationed sunlight
all the emeralds in christendom don't add up
                to a wobbly stop sign in snow
slick streets feature in my dream
                the one about Rhenish kings at scratch golf
it's a virulent mix of today and yesterday,
                layered in mud and hay, like cake
so I woke and wrote your postcard on the boulevard
                an unfortunate place where it's all explained—
the coast is clear, let's hear the studio tour
                and get the dope on blood and tears
and fear as Tonto, I notice, is frantic
                they call that the ghost dance
there's never a canary or coal mine when you need one
                and now all at once we're orphans, sore
as the bus driver shot on the top step
                or having a possible coffee
what's the diff, between death and refreshments—
                nothing stays warm for long
we pay up and go
                by the busload to bed

BULLETIN

the day as a room made of paper
above & all around

trails of snails of planes
forensic accounting

pick the beads up from the bone
at your throat
             let them fall
like birdsong along the limb of
the street's last tree

before the empty park
where trash gathers
like prisoners at a fence
to watch the living

what it is like to be dead
but have to finish
the sentence

that is all
static

INSTITUTIONAL VIEW

The silence is quiet here in Eden.
That vacuum has worked its magic.

Jamais dust on the moon rocks, thanks
to the doctor in loafers who works rooms
                              unlooming,

unknotting problems and creepy speech.
The cat's posture's better and her grades
                              shot up,

the greyhounds relax and have tossed out
                    the sleep drugs.

But being Croatian and with a big serve,
I find the med spells less than enchanting.

Give me a court with the score love to love
and I show you toujours the great escape

from gown and town. But it is egg to egg
                              out there.
Better watch your step.

PILGRIM
on the street in washington, dc

walking 15th with my blindfold tight & treasury head's
no help with directions, will not answer my scream. i do tend to
wander in the mind. my family says i'm not right in the head:
then i should be left alone—get it? i say, but they never do.
which way to go? why not i as king bee or turtle dove,
blake engraving, page on fire, anything but a white hair on god's
black bustier; beg a little something for the pain; limbs ache from
swinging at the low curves of more doubts than you can shake a
bible at, which way to vote, thumbs up or down, on derry on
gaza on comet on vixen. i pluck a piece of 3rd avenue el out of
my scalp & wing it at all maos jesuses & e. e. cummings-es.
which way to live? while angels meringue on pinheads i
wade out to wait for the light & bob & bing now swing my way
got up in blue, they help me off the sawhorse I copped & say,
don't block the limos of justice. my ride ends in their eyes:
petition for asylum denied.
so hell they lead me to shore & grin & now i must begin
again. the sawhorse stays hungry & alone.

SCENE FROM A BUS

deep image will not work in shallows
                        here lies some version of eyes Islip just
a distraction from the broken slope of shoulder
                                   cracked old hills
the lady drinks Poland Springs
                   like hope eternal
                            Wall Street's a week away
who gets to touch the creamery or thighs not
    the Scottsboro Boys again they rise in front of my car
in dark in deep in dark in deep
                    a bell's a ringing fire
                             this is not a mural
a breast pokes from a rug of graves
              the breast full of sand
                  the graves like beds unmade
in faraway Queens where the cross streets rule
                     is a thumb in the eye
my fate or yours no I insist
             after you come only
                 the last of the red hot pokers
like a limo of brokers
             a torture encrusted with silver so
                I can't see for miles anymore
it's terminally official
             I sleep in a drawer like a vaudeville baby
                   waiting for my big break
                       to break

OFF BROADWAY

All the world's a stage. So
if the globe's a show,
then
        British bomber on Guanxiu hill.
Ribs, rocks. Water somewhere near.
Left alone, the ox.
               A grocery store
in Nyack. Pork roast on the stove
at home, a mauve sweat suit
without sweat.
           Off stage a voice.
Setting a scene, with directions. Night.
day. May. Right whale. Nails. How
can you play this sheet music, this
blanket music, sounds woolly in
the ear then clear.
           Make the bed. All
the world's a bed. Flowers open and turn.
Stop me if you've heard this. In New York
and China people eat, scream, bleed, see.
What else is there. More scenes. Flats.
Actors.
       And always left on, the ghost light.
A way of saying. Keep moving in near-dark,
the only faith, to get us to the bigger light,
which is or isn't in opening night.

note: ghost light is a small lamp kept continuously lit on stage in
a dark theater

REAL ESTATE

The land is steaming. An agent drives a stake in. The feeling, ancient age on its knees.

In spruce and oak a last gasp, a mating of weights and measures.

Spirit level says yes to hammer, to fields skeletal with erection. The ribs wait in warm rain.

Around a house, a bigger house. Hands swarm over the earth, making place, room by room, tomb by tomb.

BACKSEAT DRIVER

White lobster with blonde hair
in the porthole of Harold Lloyd glasses.
Wear-care, pay attention to brakes,
she thinks, dreamily piloting a silent
submersible through Cleveland suburbs.

Do not be afraid of monsters or of being
alone, he idles, at a stop light.

Go ahead & cry, be a werewolf or a low cloud.
Test the waters, assess the pressure.
How low can you go?

There is a map with tear stains, music
you heard, sketched pedestrians,
notes on grammar, signposts;
a land becoming text under all
the atmospheres, a depth weighing
on you, its push to act smart,
to bring home trophies to Pepper Pike
Ohio, the ziggurats by Erie with
welcome mats of burnished cold.

This: yourself & husband on your big
trip, on roads that swell & harden,
or roll out like tongue to the lip
of horizon. To the left a motocross
race, to the right Troy smoldering.

Straight ahead, broken teeth &
heavy breathing. Terra incognita
a dog, almost, made it across.
Stop at the body: a pointer.
The path, across the back
of an old hand.

MANHATTAN SUTRA

I'm having this thought about place
paradise for a day's the deal
of a lifetime as a matador locks
the park behind him (beret *olé*)
                                now
some guy is bringing my car
but can keep it I've had it & *basta*
get me kabul with krispy kreme
a large with milk (yes milk)
diamonds and elk in the drink

& ask if we have a reservation—
honey, you bet & are on it
my goal now return with less time
I'll show you where poets go
to die in the museum of the city
                          of New York
he rose from the bar with a diaper
                                  dusting the dust—
same again with a twist?

STILL LIFE WITH INSOMNIA & TOKYO

cannot sleep in any time zone
even Claudio Stampi's research &
licking someone's toes in a wish
become winks adding to 40 &
not snoring—a game of squash
gin blossoms & Monte Cassino assault
wake up driver, it's my stop—
                    the futon store &
a play by Dr. Noh ("Yes We Have No Piranhas")—
                now restlessness leads me west
to a land grab, a naval battle with macaques
marimba mallets, warm milk & cookies—
          then ninja conductors lead the bullet train
          in Nissan's 9th Symphony
music washes over like the baths of my cat mother—
clean, wet, & sleek-furred *inamora* I beg to rejoin
my bed in the underworld with Yomiuri Giants
all getting Zs, how else would they grow
               but I cannot write a straight line
crossing the median for a wreck with a truck
road snowed with feathers & me in orbit
with The Otter & obscure constellations until
some bratty comet vomits beer &
planetary gagging drags me to bright surface
polished as lakes
         & the sad sight of sun up & raring to fry
another day to go for those already in line
with steady rested eyes &
         I cry & sue for peace please I surrender
         too tired to attack
         while Japan naps

note: *inamora*—present but not fully awake (Japanese)

EASTER IN THE HORSE LATITUDES (Capriccio)

A fiftieth birthday like calmed ships, the ocean smooth
as abdomens, a hundreth made of video, twice,
the thousandth by doctors locked in cells.

In the mud of Serbia, among Somalia's khat women.
The roots of grass.

Here,
this Sacramento field where brown hands pull
from their sleep the deep vegetables
& someone
                    walks among them
offering balm from a torn shirt, an arm reaching
out with a little rouge, fruit colors.

Today the 2000th attempt to forgive & this walking
is among guns, the rusted hulls of every thing
wrecked, bones of bones stirring dirt, as names
rain down, the names of all unable to straighten
under the day's weight, under wind that is
something pleading. Flowers, breath,

an eye unafraid of water's soft belly
that closes, dying to go home.

PURE WORD
for RK

Halve an orange. Inside, dynamite. Outside, white paper.

There is decoration in the earth, eaten at edges,
whole whales of physics and traffic.

Deliver babies of softest vowel.
Sail loft, a hammock of cloud, condor,
the world river of selfless green,
glass hill, planet of hands, and always Florida.
Butter, gears, weeds, speech.

Then clotted potential, a wing torn: why it walks where it is
going,
the layers of cur on the bias, a cost of fur, cold spine.

So plant a berry, the heart book. Bury.
And.

Now, unsound.

Hear no more the time, sage, rosemary.

AUBADE

magnolia gleams like a tree of tongues
someone on a porch bangs boards
this Sunday city where even air hisses

I sleep with a painter to get whites whiter
last night was Manhattan & navigation combined
today looks more like a wall

this is going nowhere
but *that* is another story

SARGASSO SEA

Shoes like drowning mouths

Sidewalk sky round
hole of a jar
on a hill

I am saying something here
find your own corner
whore

I wish I had glasses
half full or half empty

No roses
No soap

My love lies bleeding
bleeding o lord thou
kayoed with one punch

What do a zoo and a Maori tattoo
have in common
You

I predict the winner
You guess of what
Together we are a science
or bible

Sails belly somewhere
Here the calm is killing me

SEPARATION ANXIETY

> *the self is an other*
> Jorie Graham and Arthur Rimbaud

she says I want your child
      but really is after what comes
between us the poet knows
      I live inside her camped
on heights in the mint I wait
      but see the valley widen
like eyes as waters divide
      the world (how it goes
one for you & one for me)
      she eats a green apple
& my tongue is bitter

      & finally & together we make
in the grass two places for her
      to sleep & long after everything
ends in the night we laugh
      & weep & weep

PUNCH AND JUDY

Objects on the sill, white
like the sill.
The curtain is white

Behind, bottle green outside
the window.

A tall cup broad at the top, narrowing down,
a low wide plastic box,

the mug steaming,
the box half open,
unable to close, broken.
The leaves trembling.

This is where you come in.

STILL LIFE WITH GUILT

A hydrant is red as Stalingrad.
Around it is only stalling.

You dream
an infanta cradling skinned hare or greyhound.

Rain is a snow of glass.
Sweep up pieces and lick the blood on a hand,
on hands.

The cleaning unending.

DREAM FRAGMENT

Morning or evening is steered by Ahabs burning earth in search
                                        of the white
sale, & a confused foot alone in the sweaty cell of shoes
                        & how to wake when a grave tree
steps away from the race
                hoping for adoption by a gay couple of decades
before swimming where there are no arms
                        only fish glittering like leaves as they sift
toward the dark summer at the bottom of the heart

COLD SPRING

But you know how to pray to God. Tell them, 'C'est fini!'
I will not repeat the story of my ancestors, of my past, of
the devil.
      Yemba Shinga

the sun
again loud
fights to the bottom here
& dead cars oiled with light
live

& a pale face
rises to the bus growing
bright over black road

as a comb in dark damp hair
reaches shoulders
like shore

& eyes close
& now clear as day see
seeds
blink open
on earth

LAUGHING SUTRA

Teach me the meaning of monopolistic intent,
that my lawyers may avoid heavy fines.
Forever unfolding like a bolt of cloth,
a suit in time saves nine.
                              Aim first for sky
to show solemn thought, then drop book on foot.
                    Marry a military governor
to occupy his terrain. Drive your mechanic
home from your date.
            Buddha said this, and that,
always going on about nothing.